A
Culinary
Passage
Through
India

A Recipe From Every Region of India

Steven Heap

DEAR READER

This book is dedicated to the good people of India and to be fortunate enough to be able to take advantage of the airline companies that offer affordable flights to visit India. Sometimes the most interesting paths we can take in life are due to the subtle and inadvertent actions of others that innocently inspire us and help us develop our own consciousness and understanding of what was once unknown. Just as the evolution of Indian food has developed over the past 8000 years and is now one of the most distinct foods recognisable globally and a phenomenon which occurred unintentionally but still triumphant which is a similar story to the writing of this book.

It is true in its form, written and cooked in the home, inspired by years of research, travel and passion. Nothing professional, no gloss, no gimmicks, not even a proper camera, editor, publisher nor designer (Whoop! Thanks Krystopf Markowski for the cover design!). But still an effective book, home-grown in every sense but inspired from what is out there, what I have seen, what I know, what I want to know more of, and what I want to share with you! The infinite joys of Indian food!

HAPPY COOKING!

ISBN: 9798699404087

Index

RECIPES OF THE NORTHERN REGION

RECIPES OF THE WESTERN REGION

RECIPES OF THE SOUTHERN REGION

RECIPES OF THE CENTRAL REGION

RECIPES OF THE EASTERN REGION

RECIPES OF THE NORTH EASTERN REGION

INDIAN FOOD

India has the second largest population in the world filled with a wide range of geographical landscapes. From the Himalayan mountain chain in the North, the Thar Desert in the North-West down to the South with its tropical coastlines. Given the diversity in soil, climate, culture, ethnic groups and occupations combined with the availability of local ingredients, Indian food has a staggering range of flavours and regional dishes that have been shaped over 8000 years.

It may be surprising that approximately 30% of all ingredients we recognise in Indian cuisine where introduced by the outside world in one form or another. The Mongols from Central Asia came to India in the 12th century whose diet relied healthily on meat and dairy products. Followed by the Moghuls who were a Turko-Persian people who brought their royal kitchens with them filled with rich aromatic dishes consisting of saffron, milk, cream, nuts, dried fruit, samosa, pilaus, butter and cream. It is no surprise that the Moghuls only ate once a day and that their cuisine inevitably influenced the dishes of Northern India which we now know as Mughlai cuisine.

Dishes such as dhansak, korma, passanda, haleem, rogan josh all reflect the cooking styles which were introduced by the Parsis who arrived in the 8th Century, who originated in Persia (modern day Iran). These dishes are mostly meat based as the Parsis generally regarded vegetables as poor man's food. The Parsis also introduced the tandoor oven which gave birth to 'tikka' dishes and 'naan' which is the Persian word for bread.

The Portuguese landed in India in 1498 and introduced New World ingredients such as chillies, chicken, potatoes, tomatoes, peanuts and guava. Vindaloo is probably the most iconic Indo-Portuguese dish. 'Vin' means wine, 'alho' means garlic in Portuguese.

When the British colonized India (referred to as the Raj, 1858 – 1947), India was by far the richest country on earth at the time. The British merely introduced cauliflower and orange carrots but what the British gained from India is immense in terms of food alone.

British India was controlled by the East India Company and at the time also comprised of modern day Bangladesh, and Pakistan which was founded in 1947 and the area of Bengal became Bangladesh in 1971. This is why many restaurants of Pakistani or Bangladeshi origin still refer to themselves as Indian restaurants today as they were all part of the one country for generations and share a common food culture.

Under the British Raj, approximately 30 million Indians left to work overseas in predominantly commonwealth countries and obviously took their seeds and cooking habits with them. Some of the countries included in the Indian diaspora are; Kenya, Uganda, Malaysia, Singapore, Trinidad and Tobago, Belize, Surinam, Burma (modern day Myanmar), Jamaica, South Africa and of course Britain. This colossal movement of people introduced Indian food to the larger world and new dishes were created out of the local ingredients.

It is understandable that the British that went to India over the centuries became accustomed to local tastes and also spread this amazing cuisine around the world in the form of curry powder which was created so that the when British went back to Britain they could continue eating the flavours they had become addicted to. So much so, even the former enemies of Britain incorporated Indian influenced food into their eating habits. Even today the Japanese Navy still has curry on their menu every Friday and the Germans have their curry wurst (curried sausages).

Chicken tikka masala is *even* one of Britain's national dishes! In all, Indian food is one of the most versatile and widespread cuisines and due to the many cooking styles, variations, ingredient flexibility and popularity it is still continuing to evolve. Indian food can be vegan, vegetarian, meaty, fragrant, mild, spicy, sweet or bitter and no matter what your tastes, religion, rich or poor, Indian food offers something for absolutely everyone. The recipes in this book take India food back to its roots where it all began.

Religious Dietary Requirements

Combined with the sheer availability of food, Indian cuisine has also been shaped by a myriad of religious influences and historical events such as invasions, trade-relations and dynasties which have all shaped its diet. As the following recipes are authentic to each region it may be interesting to summarise the dietary guidelines for each of the following major religions of India.

Hindu

About 80% of India follows the Hindu religion that is mostly vegetarian (pure vegetarian) or lacto-vegetarian (including dairy products). A minority of Hindus do eat eggs, fish, poultry and goat or lamb but as they believe in karma, animals are killed as quickly and as painlessly as possible. The cow is considered a sacred animal so the consumption of beef is strictly prohibited.

The Hindu caste system is often a contributor to what foods are eaten. Brahmins for example, who are at the top of the Indian caste system particularly in Southern Indian refrain from eating onions and garlic but many will eat meat and often include hing/asafoetida (a pungent tree sap which fried it hot oil and has an onion aroma) in their dishes as a substitute. That being said, other people from different religions also use hing as a flavouring in addition to onion and garlic.

Islam

Islam is the second most prominent religion in Indian comprising of around 18% of the population. All meat besides pork, which is Haram (forbidden) can be eaten but it has to be Halal (slaughtered in accordance with Islamic law).

Sikhism

Some Sikhs refrain from meat and eggs but when meat is eaten, Halal meat is forbidden. As the cow is not sacred in Sikhism, beef is eaten although rarely. Only lacto-vegetarian food is served at temples.

Buddhism

Buddhists generally refrain from killing anything that is alive but many Buddhists voluntarily eat what they wish. Their diet ranges from being very strict vegan, to lacto-vegan and omnivore but food served at Buddhist temples is strictly vegan.

Jainism

Jains follow a very strict diet which is devoutly vegan which aims to ensure the preservation of Karma. To avoid injury to even the smallest of animals many Jains refrain from eating some root vegetables, honey, yeast, mushrooms, and often avoid eating leafy vegetables. Onions and garlic are forbidden as they are thought to invigorate the libido. Food has to be eaten on the day it is prepared and never to be stored overnight as it may harvest micro-organisms and even water should be filtered before consumption.

ABOUT THE RECIPES

Compiling the recipes for this book was no easy feat. Each region has so much to offer in terms of its cuisine. Choosing the most iconic dish was pretty straight forward for some regions and far more challenging for others, particularly in practical terms, for instance, some recipes call for ingredients almost impossible to find outside of a certain region. Therefore, the recipes are all compiled of ingredients that most people *by and large* can access. There are a few instances where suggestions or alternatives are made. The recipes have also been carefully selected to provide a balance of meat, vegetarian, poultry and seafood dishes.

Each of the recipes are based on approximately 2 servings, each serving consisting of 250 grams of the *main ingredient* (vegetables, lamb, fish, etc) for each person.

Recipe Abbreviations

Grams – **g**

Millilitres – **ml**

1000ml – **1 litre**

Teaspoon – **tsp**

Tablespoon – **tbsp**

1 cup – **235 ml**

Inch – **"**

For the 2 kebab recipes; **190 degrees centigrade/ 375 degrees Fahrenheit**. Or **3 inches/7.5cms** above hot coals if using a barbeque.

Scaling Up Recipes

Of course recipes can be scaled up for more servings, however, it is recommended to scale up the 'spices' by only around 50%. In other words, if a dish requires 10 red dried chillies for two servings, if you wanted to make that dish for 10 servings, use 25 and not 50.

Recipe Variations

There are no 'official' recipes for any dish. The ingredients used and even the cooking techniques differ between households (or restaurants) based on the vision and preferences of the particular cook, or the ingredients available. Even for something as simple as making chapatti you can find countless variations of a recipe. And, of course you can literally invent dishes and change recipes/methods where ever you see fit.

The ingredients necessary to prepare Indian food can be staggering in volume especially in terms of herbs and spices. Many of the recipes in this book inevitably require a large variety of ingredients to create the dishes to optimum level. If you find that your pantry does not allow for all the ingredients to cook a particular dish you can leave out ingredients if necessary. Or, if you don't like the taste of a particular ingredient simply omit it.

COOKING INDIAN FOOD

The five Flavours

When cooking a balanced and authentic Indian dish it is important to consider the 5 types of tastes, most of which have been incorporated into all the recipes in this book. The 5 flavours are; Sweet, Sour, Salty, Bitter and Umani (savoury or meaty).

Cooking Techniques

Indian dishes often use a combination of 3 to 6 cooking techniques to prepare a single dish but most of the processes are also apparent in the cooking of other national cuisines.

Blending/Grinding

You will need a food processor/food blender to make certain pastes, garam masala, and also for making ginger & garlic paste, although you can finely chop your ginger and garlic if you wish, or you can even add the spices whole without grinding them. When grinding whole spices into powders, it is best to grind them as finely as possible as this gives the spice a bigger surface area and ensures a superior flavour, with the exemption of grinding spices for kebabs, where a grainier more rustic texture is generally preferred.

Par-Boiling

Several recipes require some par-boiling (partial boiling). This means to boil your ingredient/s, usually vegetables like potatoes until they are about 70% cooked and then drain them to be added to the dish to cook the remaining 30% so they absorb flavours. It is recommended to add a pinch of salt and turmeric in the boiling water. The drained water can be used as stock/additional water to add to a dish while cooking.

Dry Roasting

Certain ingredients like whole spices for making garam masala and green chillies can be dry roasted before blending into a powder or paste. Simply add the ingredients to a dry pan and gently heat them up until you can smell their aroma which is when their essential oils are released. This can take around 2-5 minutes depending on the temperature. Once roasted, allow them to cool down before blending. In India, many cooks only roast whole spices for meat dishes, for vegetarian dishes they often do not roast the spices before blending with the exception of garam masala. Try experimenting to find your preference.

Sauté – To fry something briefly on a high temperature.

Boil – To cook something in water with a rapid temperature so the water bubbles.

Simmering – To boil something on a medium/gentle flame so *it* cooks evenly.

Tarka/Tadka/Bhoona – The technique of tempering oil with various spices and adding it on top of a finished dish for garnish and added flavour.

Preparation

It is not rare when cooking Indian food to have dozens of ingredients on the kitchen table or work tops waiting to be marinated, blended, roasted, ground, chopped etc. The preparation of the ingredients can often take longer to prepare than cooking the actual dish. Good preparation practices will get you the best dishes.

Reduction

Reduction is a cooking method used when boiling or simmering a dish which allows water to evaporate which thickens sauces and intensifies flavour.

Sealing

Frying meat/poultry at a high temperature in oil to brown the edges slightly which *seals* the meat so that juices are not lost in the cooking process which creates a improved and more intense flavour.

Caramelisation

Caramelisation is a cooking method caused by the heat accumulated on the sides of a cooking pan which causes the oxidation of sugar that creates a brown colour particularly when cooking ginger & garlic, onions, or a wet sauce. Ingredients that have been caramelized produce a more intense flavour.

Splitting the Oil

The process of splitting the oil is a valuable step when making a wet curry. Most dishes begin with heating oil in a pan and then gradually adding ingredients, for example, dry ingredients first and then the ingredients that contain moisture later (such as tomatoes, yogurt, cream), or even water to thin out sauces to prolong the cooking time. Once you have a combination of oil and water, there is a certainty that the oil will rise to the surface of the sauce in the cooking process. This is important because in ensures that the ingredients in the dish are no longer absorbing any more moisture *thus* indicating they are fully cooked. The oil splitting usually occurs either quickly on high heat, or around 5-8 minutes on a moderate heat. A good tip is to cook your dish on a high heat for some time and then turn the heat down to a simmer towards the end of the cooking stage which helps the oil to split.

Temperature

The temperature that dishes cook at is dependent on several factors; what stage the dish is at, for example, when tempering spices in hot oil it is best to use a moderate heat to allow the spices to cook out and extract as much flavour into the oil as possible. Or when frying onions, the longer they fry for the better the taste. Frying/browning onions never produces good results in terms of flavour if the temperature is too high. You will achieve a far better taste and colour if onions are cooked slowly.

Frying ginger & garlic should also be done a moderate heat so they caramelise slightly which ensures the raw flavour has been cooked out. Also, burning the garlic will ruin the taste your dish and turn it bitter so remember to cook garlic slowly.

Once the onions, ginger & garlic are cooked it'll be time to add the powdered spices. Again, these need cooking out properly to extract the flavours so they should be cooked on a moderate heat as they can burn easily. A good tip if your pan is dry/very hot when adding powdered spices is to add a little water to reduce the temperature slightly and prolong the cooking time to capture the most of their flavour.

When adding meat and poultry to your pan you can turn up the temperature to *seal* (fry until slightly brown on the edges) and then turn the heat down to a simmer so that the meat cooks thoroughly.

Pans & Cooking Utensils

To follow the recipes in this book are very simple in terms of kitchen utensils. All you will need is a frying pan, cooking pot with a lid for boiling and a tava/flat crepe pan for making rotis. As well as a knife, chopping board and a sieve from draining rice etc.

Lids

Using a lid on your pan retains heat in your dishes as they are cooking as lids do not allow any steam to leave. It is beneficial to use a lid when either adding meats or raw vegetables to a dish as they will cook more quickly and evenly. However, using a lid on the pan is the *opposite* of reduction.

The Dum Method

The dum method is when you put a lid on your pan and seal it with fresh dough. This is a traditional way of cooking that originated in Rajasthan, a very dry semi-desert region where fire wood was scarce and the cooks had to make use of every available bit of heat from the fire. The dum method works well with biryani and meat dishes, but a pressure cooker is the modern version, or even a pan with a tight fitting lid is sufficient.

Cooking Time & Reconstituting

A good trick when making curries is to turn the heat off when a dish is about 95% cooked. Once the heat is turned off the ingredients still continue to cook. This is particularly true when making rice which will continue to steam long after draining.

When a curry is in the final stages of cooking, it can often look pretty liquidy. The moment you turn the heat off, the curry will rest and dry out slightly so bear this in mind to achieve the correct consistency of your curries for serving.

Allowing food to relax a little after cooking allows for a slightly more intense flavour as the juices absorb into the ingredients. That is why if you leave a curry over night in the refrigerator many people believe that it tastes better the next day. 'Next day' curries will probably need to be reconstituted when they are heated up again by adding enough water to achieve the desired consistency.

Adding Water & Cooking Raw Flavours Away

It's always a good idea to have a cup of water to hand when cooking. Your pan may get very hot and risk burning your ingredients; by simply adding a little water cools things down, particularly when you add semi wet ingredients like ginger & garlic paste, or when powdered spices are added.

Adding a little water can stop your garlic from burning or help mix your powdered spices and prevent them from burning. Adding water also prolongs the cooking process, which is important, as cooking your spices properly gives a better flavour to the overall dish. The same can be said about tomatoes which have a raw taste unless they are thoroughly cooked through. Water also allows for the caramelisation which builds up on the sides of the pan during the cooking process. This caramelisation should be scraped back into a dish while stirring which adds additional flavour.

Marinating & Tenderising

Some of the recipes call for a marination time of 3 hours but for best results it is better to marinate overnight. For tougher meats such as lamb on the bone you could add a teaspoon of tendorising powder to the marinade. Tendoriser is a white powder containing an extract from the papaya fruit which contains an enzyme called *papain* which helps to break down proteins and ensures a soft texture to your meat once cooked. Similarly, pineapple juice is a good alternative.

After marinating your ingredients remember to also add any remaining marinade paste to the dish, along with what you marinated. Marinating is optional if you have less time to prepare a dish that requires marination but the resulting taste will not be quite as good.

Soaking Lentils & Pulses

When soaking lentils to make dal dishes, how long they are soaked depends on what variety of lentil you are using. Smaller lentils such as urid, moong, masor, toor or split red can be soaked for as little as an hour. Lentils and pulses with a skin on them such as dried kidney beans or chana dal (dried halved chickpeas) should be soaked overnight.

Lentil should be washed before soaking to remove any grit or particles. In this way, you can then use the water they were soaked in to cook with as a stock.

Also, adding a pinch or two of bicarbonate of soda to the water speeds up the absorption process. Once the lentils have been soaked you can simply boil them in a pan of water until soft with a little salt and turmeric, or you can use a pressure cooker to soften them more quickly.

Resting

Once a dish has been cooked it is recommended to allow it to rest for about 10 minutes. This will help the ingredients soak up even more of the flavours.

Chopping Techniques

The recipes call for a wide range of different styles of chopping/slicing.

Coarsely Chopped – Roughly chopped.

Diced – Cubed.

Julienne – Cut into long thin uniformed strips similar to matchsticks/batons, often used for garnish and presentation.

Shredded – Similar to julienne but more coarsely chopped.

Textures

There are generally 4 different textures of sauce. Which texture you aim to achieve is a matter of preference.

Smooth, Dry *or* Wet (Masala)

To make a smooth sauce simple use ground/powdered spices. Cut the onions very finely or even grate (burji) them and generally avoid any lumpy ingredients.

A wet sauce can be achieved by simply adding more water. For a drier sauce simply allow all the moisture in a sauce to reduce/ evaporate by cooking on a moderate temperature. However, wet curries go better with rice and are great for dipping into with rotis.

Grainy

Cooking grainy or rustic curries can be achieved by adding ingredients that are coarsely chopped, such as the onions, split chillies and whole spices.

INGREDIENTS

From reading the previous chapter you should now have a good understanding of some of the essential cooking methods and tips to creating awesome Indian food. Merely obtaining a recipe for a dish and following it will not necessarily achieve optimum cooking results. To achieve great cooking results it is important to understand the dynamics of the ingredients you are using. In this way, you will not only get better results from the recipes, you will also become a better independent cook.

Whole & Powdered Spices

Whole spices are fried in hot oil to temper/season/flavour the oil, either at the beginning of the cooking process or, to create a *tarka* which is poured on top of a finished dish at the end of the cooking process to provide added flavour.

Whole spices can also be ground into a powder in varying quantities to produce spice mixes including garam masala. Grinding spices into powder from whole will always give a superior taste compared to using packaged/store bought powders. Try blending your own whole coriander and cumin into powder for the recipes for a superior flavour.

Green Cardamom

When using whole green cardamom, crack the husks with a knife or kitchen scissors so that the small black interior seeds that contain the majority of the flavour are dispersed into the dish while cooking.

Black Cardamom

Black cardamom is not related to green cardamom although they share a common name. It has a pungent smoky taste and can be ground in various spice mixes or added whole to hot oil and is generally used to flavour meat dishes.

Cassia Bark & Cinnamon

There are several species of cinnamon, 'Cinnamomum verun' is known as true cinnamon, or Sri Lankan cinnamon which is light brown in colour and has a flaky cigar-like appearance which breaks apart in the cooking process. Sri Lankan cinnamon is best for making garam masala. There is also 'cinnamomum cassia' which is dark brown and tougher so does not break apart when fried is favourable for the recipes in this book as is referred to as *cassia bark*.

Turmeric

All mentions of turmeric in the recipes refer to powdered turmeric.

Fresh Coriander

Fresh Coriander can be used in Indian food in many ways. Either for chutneys, as a garnish, or chopped and added to dishes towards the end of the cooking process. Most of the flavour is contained in the stalks which are best for making chutneys or finely slicing and adding to sauces and rice dishes. Coriander leaves have a subtle flavour and their beautiful colour is perfect for garnishing but remember to chop it at the last minute as it wilts quickly.

Bay Leaves & Tej Patta

Many recipes call for the use of bay leaves. There are generally two types of bay leaves that can be used. Standard bay leaves can be found world-wide and are generally considered the Mediterranean type which have an oregano/thyme-like aroma, and there is another kind called *tej patta*, which is the leaf of the cinnamon tree and tastes mildly of cinnamon. You can use either for all recipes.

Asafoetida/Hing

As mentioned earlier, asafoetida is also known as hing and is usually found in powdered form in small tubs. If you are not able to find hing powder when shopping do not worry, you can simply leave it out of the recipe.

Kasuri Methi

Kasuri methi is the sun dried leaves of the fenugreek plant. It is widely used in Indian dishes especially in the North. It is used to flavour gravies and is applied to dishes by scrunching it up between the fingers and discarding any tough stalks before adding it to a dish.

Curry Leaves

Curry leaves, also known as 'sweet neem' are very common in South Indian recipes. The give dishes a distinctive aroma and taste, and ideally fresh leaves are used as the dried variety lack flavour. However, depending on where you live they may be very difficult to get hold of. Although it is best to use them when a recipe requires them, it will not make too much difference if you leave them out of the dish.

Jaggery

Jaggery is unrefined cane sugar although it can also be made from various palms. Several recipes require jaggery but if you don't have any you can simply use ordinary sugar.

Vinegar

Several recipes require the use of vinegar. The most common type of vinegar used in India is white vinegar but you can use most ordinary vinegars you have to hand, or even substitute the vinegar with either lemon or lime juice.

Tomatoes

Tomatoes are an important ingredient in many curries. Ideally, it is best to use fresh tomatoes that have been chopped finely so they disintegrate in the cooking process (or you could blend them into a paste in a food processor before cooking if you want a smoother sauce). When choosing fresh tomatoes it is important to choose the ripest tomatoes you can find. Ripe tomatoes contain more sugar and less starch than harder unripe tomatoes and have a great red colour.

However, you can substitute fresh tomatoes with tinned tomatoes and if so, it's a good idea to blend them into a smooth paste in a food processor before cooking. You can even use tomato puree/paste as an alternative. Simply add 1 part paste to 2 parts water and stir to mix well.

If using fresh tomatoes, they generally need to be cooked until they break down or as many of the recipes describe as 'disintegrate'. As tomato skin does not disintegrate it's always best to cut the tomatoes quite small so your dishes do not end up with visible pieces of tomato skin. Cutting fresh tomatoes finely also allows them to break down faster when cooking.

Oil

Most Indian dishes require a certain amount of oil at the early stage of cooking or as a 'tarka'. Standard neutral oils such as vegetable, rapeseed or sunflower are fine to use, however, for some dishes using various other oils produces a better flavour. For example, for green leafy dishes or kebabs, mustard oil can be used for a more pungent and authentic flavour. To prepare mustard oil ready for cooking simply heat it up to smoking point which burns away the *erucic acid* as some studies have found it to be detrimental to health in high doses. Then turn the heat down to cooking temperature.

Ghee or clarified butter is often used for many dishes to give a more authentic and more intense flavour. Ghee and mustard oil have a lower smoking point than vegetable or sunflower oil, and thus gives a roasted and slightly nutty flavour. Before adding any ingredient to oil, make sure that the oil has reached cooking temperature.

Coconut oil is used predominantly in the Southern regions of India. You can use coconut oil for any of the dishes listed in the Southern Region recipes in this book. If that is the case, it is worthwhile to spend a little more money on 'extra virgin coconut oil' which is far tastier than regular coconut oil.

The amount of oil or *type* used for each recipe is a matter of personal preference. The quantity of oil in each recipe serves as a guideline. It is true that oil carries the flavours and also adds a glossy sheen to the finished dish.

Flour

Rice Flour

Rice flour can be used for thickening sauces. It can be dry roasted in a pan until browned to increase the warm taste of the rice. A tablespoon or two of rice flour can also be added to batter when making pakora, pokada and bhaji which helps the batter stay crispier for longer after deep frying. You could equally use plain flour if you wish.

Atta

When making various Indian breads 'atta' (whole-wheat) flour is mostly used. There are different coarsenesses available from white, fine, coarse and brown. Which one you use depends on your preference.

Gram Flour

Gram flour, also known as besan or chickpea flour is used for pakoras, pakodis and bhajis (deep fried battered Indian snacks), and for thickening or flavouring sauces. If a recipe requires roasted gram flour, simply heat a dry pan and add the flour and stir constantly until the flour has turned a darker colour. Roasting gram flour creates a warmer flavour and cooks away the raw taste.

Meat, Poultry and Seafood

Chicken

Chicken is always cooked with the skin off in Indian food. Some prefer to cook chicken on the bone for added flavour as the juices from the marrowbone seep into the sauce but you can also cook it off the bone if you wish.

Lamb & Mutton

The words lamb and mutton can be confusing. In the West, mutton refers to older sheep meat but in many countries mutton can also refer to goat. Both lamb and goat can be used interchangeably in all the recipes. Cooking lamb/mutton on the bone gives a superior taste but you can equally use boneless if you prefer and cut it into bite sized pieces.

Fish

As you can see from the pictures of the fish recipes, the 'darne cut' is preferred but is optional. The darn cut not only avoids wasting any part of the fish through filleting but also allows more flavour by including the bone which also holds the fish together while cooking.

Some prefer to fry the fish after it has been marinated to seal in the flavours and get a firmer texture while others simply add the raw fish to the dish and cook in within the sauce, it's all a matter of preference.

Prawns

Prawns can either be thawed out from frozen or de-shelled and de-veined from fresh. Prawns cook very quickly so three and half minutes of cooking time is sufficient. If prawns are overcooked they will have a rubbery texture. It is suggested to marinate prawns before cooking with a pinch of salt, turmeric and a dash of either lemon or lime juice. Prawns can be marinated for between 30 minutes or up to an hour depending on the size of the prawns.

Diary

Yogurt

It is recommended to use 'full fat' plain natural yogurt and avoid low fat varieties than can split when added to hot sauces as low fat yogurt has a high water content. A plain, set, thick or Greek style yogurt is ideal for Indian food.

Paneer

Paneer is a popular Indian cheese made by boiling full fat milk with either vinegar or lemon juice so the curds and whey split. The curds are then placed into muslin cloth so they whey can drain away then and pressed over night with a flat and heavy object which will form a firm cheese block. Paneer does not melt so remains whole in the cooking process. It can be braised (shallow fried to form a caramelised texture) before it is added to a dish or simply chopped into the desired shape beforehand. The hotter the paneer gets, the softer the texture.

Souring

Many Indian dishes require some form of souring agent. Some of the recipes call for either lime or lemon juice and for Southern recipes tamarind is often used. You can purchase tamarind blocks from most of the major supermarkets which contains seeds which need to be taken out before using. Better still you can also find it in convenient bottles that do not contain seeds. Actually, the type of sour ingredient you add is optional and a matter of personal preference. Ingredients that will also give a sour element to you dishes are as follows; plain yogurt, black salt, kokum and chaat masala.

Salt

As with most cooking, salt plays a very important role in the overall taste of a dish, especially with Indian food with its vast range of spices. Each spice tastes differently from one another and the use of salt is important to balance these flavours out.

Although salt is an acquired taste, and hence all the recipes in this book recommend using 'salt to taste'. The amount of salt used will differ between cooks. Try cooking a dish without adding salt and then taste it! This is how you are going to know how much salt to use.

Salt can also do wonders to the ingredients during the cooking process. By adding salt to onions during cooking helps the onions cook evenly and slow down the browning process which brings out a superior flavour of the onions. Adding salt also draws moisture of out ingredients.

However, if you add salt at the beginning of a dish to assist in a cooking process, it will be vitally important to check the taste of a dish for salt once it has been cooked and add additional salt if required.

Salt increases the boiling point of water so if you ever want to boil water faster, add the salt once the water has boiled.

There are many different types of salt available on the market from table/regular, black, rock/kosher or Himalayan. Of course, you could use any, but Himalayan salt contains many essential minerals and gives a superb taste to food.

Chillies

Most Indian food dishes require various forms of chillies. Either in powdered form, whole dried chillies and/or fresh green chillies. Each form of these chillies serves a different purpose. Green chillies should be added to a dish early to soften and allow their acidity to disperse throughout the dish. If you want to use green chillies for their acidity/heat you can add them whole or split and discard them when you eat the dish. Dried red chillies are either used for spice blends or tempering hot oil.

Hot Chilli Powder – Hot, a matter of preference.

Chilli Powder – Moderately hot usually blended from several chilli types.

Cayenne Pepper – Moderately hot and fruity, although referred to as pepper, it is actually a chilli powder.

Dried Red Chillies – Used for spice blends or tempering hot oil.

Kashmiri Chilli Powder – Mild to moderately hot, used for colour.

Deggi Mirch - Mildly hot, used for colour.

Paprika – Subtle flavour, sometimes sweet and used for colour.

Fresh Green – Jawala is the most common variety, moderate to hot (paste, sliced, split, roasted or whole).

Scotch Bonnet types – Habanera, Naga – Very hot, strong acidity usually scored (score the flesh in several places with a knife before cooking) & used whole.

Birds Eye – Small, hot to very hot.

Coconut

Several recipes require fresh coconut. Ideally, it is best to freshly grated coconut but if you cannot obtain any you can often find frozen grated coconut in some supermarkets. Failing that, you could use either canned coconut milk or coconut cream mixed to a paste with a little hot water.

Garnish

Recommended garnish for each dish has been left out of most recipes. Freshly chopped coriander is common followed by juliennes of ginger, sliced onion, fresh chilli or tarka. Be imaginative when garnishing your food as often a bit of garnish can make a dish look stunning.

GREEN CHUTNEY

Green chutney is a great accompaniment to many Indian foods. It is easy to make and goes great with kebabs, popodoms or for dipping fried snacks into.

Ingredients

Fresh Coriander – 1 bunch
Fresh Mint – ½ bunch (optional)
Green Chilli – 7
Fresh Ginger – 3" piece
Lemon Juice – 1 lemon
Garlic – 4 cloves
Cumin Powder – 1 tsp
Salt – to taste

Method

Blend all the ingredients in a food processor with a little water.

You can either blend it very finely or leave it slightly rustic.

GINGER & GARLIC PASTE

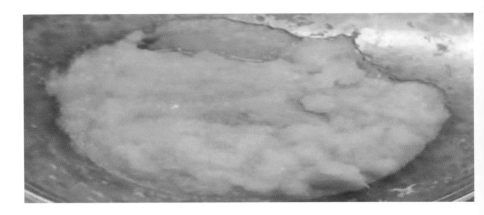

Most Indian dishes require ginger, and particularly garlic. You can blend fresh garlic and/or ginger in a food processor to make a smooth paste. You can make batches and either keep it in the fridge or store for longer periods in the freezer. Using a little bit of cooking oil in the blend will help you ginger and garlic from oxygenizing and turning a pale green colour.

The ratio of ginger to garlic is one of preference but most cooks prefer a higher proportion of garlic to ginger.

Ingredients

Method

Fresh Garlic & Fresh Ginger in a ratio of 60:40
(or, experiment to your preference)

Remove the skin from the ginger and the garlic.

Blend into a smooth paste with a food processor.

GARAM MASALA

Garam Masala literally means 'hot spices'. You could either add whole garam masala spices at the beginning of the cooking process to temper the oil, or blend the spices into a powder. Making your own garam masala will give a fresh and far superior taste to buying store bought.

Ingredients

Coriander Seed – 2 tbsp
Cumin Seed – 1.5 tbsp
Green Cardamom – 4
Cinnamon/Cassia – 1" stick
Cloves - 4
Pepper – 1 tsp
Star Anise – 1
Bay Leaf – 2
Black Cardamom – 1
Mace – 1 blade
Nutmeg – ½ pea size

Method

Dry roast all the ingredients in a dry pan on a low heat for 2-3 minutes/until aromatic. Do not allow to smoke.

Let the spices to cool down before grinding to a fine powder in a food processor.

THE DUNGHAR SMOKING TECHNIQUE

Dunghar is an ancient method of infusing dishes with a smoky taste. To use the technique, simply heat a small piece of charcoal and place in onto a small metal bowl and place the dish on top of a recipe you have just cooked. Then add a little oil or ghee to the hot charcoal and place a lid on the entire dish so that the smoke from the oiled hot charcoal is trapped and infuses the dish with a smoky flavour. You can leave the lid on the pan for around 10-15 minutes, or less for a less smoky taste. This technique works well with dal Makhani and other dal dishes but you can use the method for any dish you choose.

RECIPES OF THE

NORTHERN REGION

Bhuna Gosht

Bhuna Gosht is a popular dish in the region and is also favoured across the border in Pakistan. The slow cooking of the lamb in the spices and gravy creates a mouth watering with an incredible aroma and flavour.

Ingredients	Method

Ingredients

Lamb – 500g
Cumin Seed – 1 tbsp
Ginger & Garlic Paste – 2 tbsp
Onions – 2 (sliced)
Tomato – 5 (whole)
Green Chilli – 4 (split)
Ground Black Pepper – 1 tsp
(ground)
Turmeric – 1 tsp
Coriander Powder – 1 tbsp
Chilli Powder – 1 tsp
Bay Leaf – 2
Garam Masala – 1 tsp
Oil – 5 tbsp
Lemon Juice – ½ lemon
Salt – to taste

Method

Add oil to a pan and gently fry the cumin seed and bay leaf for 1 minute.

Brown the onions, and then add the ginger & garlic paste and fry for 2 minutes.

Add the lamb, stir well until it has sealed (approximately 7 minutes)

Add the green chilli along with all the powdered spices (not the garam masala) and salt, stir well and fry for 1 minute.

Now add the whole tomatoes and ½ cup of water, stir and bring to a boil.

Put a lid on the pan and simmer on a low flame for 1 hour 15 minutes, adding a little water occasionally if dries out.

The tomatoes will have disintegrated in the cooking process, so now carefully take out the tomato skin and discard it.

Finally, add the lemon juice and garam masala, stir and cook for a further minute.

Garwhali Kafuli

The cuisine of Uttarakhand avoids complexity but shows how simple food can be satisfying. The region is renowned for its natural beauty which is very reflected in its cuisine. Garwhali Kafuli is an easy to prepare vegetarian dish filled with fresh greens making it not only colourful but an exceptionally healthy dish. Unless you are a vegetarian this makes a great side dish to a meat main.

Ingredients

Fresh Spinach – 500g
Fresh Fenugreek Leaf – 250g
Yogurt – 1 cup
Rice Flour – 3 tbsp (dry roasted)
Coriander Powder – 1 tbsp
Turmeric – 1 tsp
Cumin Seed – 1 tsp
Green Chilli – 2
Salt – to taste
Mustard Oil – 4 tbsp

Tarka
Dried Red Chilli – 2
Black Mustard Seed – 1 tsp
Garlic – 3 cloves (coarsely chopped)
Hing – a pinch
Mustard oil – 2 tbsp

Method

Heat the mustard oil in a pan and add the coriander and fenugreek (along with their stalks) and stir-fry for a few minutes until the leaves are dark green.

Then blend the wilted leaves along with the green chilli into a smooth paste in a food processor, a few drops of water may be necessary.

Add the paste back into the same pan and bring to a boil.

Add the roasted rice flour, turmeric, coriander powder, salt and yogurt, mix well and simmer for 5 minutes.

Heat the mustard oil in a pan and slowly roast all the 'tarka' ingredients for 2-3 minutes and pour over the top of the dish to serve.

Chha Gosht

Chha Gosht translates as 'yogurt stewed lamb' and has its roots in the royal kitchens of Himachal Pradesh. It is a scrumptious and delightful dish that will make you want to cook it again and again.

Ingredients	Method
Lamb – 500g	Marinate the lamb in the yogurt, roasted gram flour, ginger & garlic paste, turmeric, coriander powder, cumin powder and salt, for 3 hours.
Onions – 2 (sliced)	
Yogurt – 2 cups	
Gram Flour – 2 tbsp (dry roasted)	
Ginger & Garlic Paste – 2 tbsp	
Turmeric – 1 tsp	Heat oil in a pan and add the bay leaf, dried red chilli, hing, cloves, cassia, green and black cardamom and gently fry for 2 minutes.
Bay Leaf – 2	
Hing – ¼ tsp	
Coriander Powder – 1.5 tbsp	
Cumin Powder – 1 tsp	
Dried Red Chilli – 4	Then add the onions and fry until golden brown.
Green Cardamom – 5	
Cloves – 4	
Cassia – 3" stick	Next, add the marinated lamb, stir well and gently simmer for 1 hour with a lid on the pan, adding a little water if the sauce dries out.
Black Cardamom - 3	
Oil – 5 tbsp	
Salt – to taste	

Dal Makhani

Punjab food has had a major influence on all Northern Indian cuisine. Da
Makhani which translates as 'butter Lentils' is one of the most flavoursome da
dishes in India and was invented by Kundan Lal Jaggi (1924 -2018) who also
invented butter chicken. The combination of various lentils, butter and cream
along with subtle spices make this dish one of the most satisfying of its kind.
The lentils and kidney beans should be soaked over-night beforehand unless
you are using canned. The soaked beans and lentils can then either be boiled in
a pressure cooker, or simply boiled until softened. The recipe requires a variety
of lentil called black gram which is simply un-shelled urid dal (which is whitish
yellow in colour).

Ingredients	Method

Ingredients

Black Gram - 1 cup
Kidney Beans – 2/3 cup
Single Cream – 70 ml
Butter – 2 tbsp
Onion – 1 large (finely chopped)
Garlic & Ginger paste – 1 tbsp
Green Chilli – to taste
Chilli Powder – to taste
Turmeric – 1 tsp
Tomato – 2 finely chopped
Cumin Seed – 1 tsp
Coriander Powder – 1 tsp
Garama masala – ½ tsp
Kasuri Methi – 1 tbsp
Oil - 3 tbsp

Method

Heat the oil in a pan and add the cumin seed until it crackles slightly, then add the onions and fry until starting to turn brown.

Then add the ginger & garlic paste and fry for 2 minutes.

Next, add the tomatoes and cook until they disintegrate, then add the powdered spices and green chillies and mix well then simmer for 1 minute.

Then add the kasuri methi, kidney beans and black gram along with the water they were cooked in and bring to a boil.

Add the butter and cream and simmer for a further 5 minutes.

Garnish with a knob of butter and a swirl of cream. Amritsa Kulcha (see page 113) is the perfect accompaniment.

Kadai Paneer

The food of Haryana is similar to its neighbouring Punjab. Kadai Paneer, also known as shahi (royal) paneer is a deliciously rich Indian cheese (paneer) dish with a thick gravy made from cashew nuts, tomatoes, cream and an elaborate array of spices.

Ingredients	Method
Paneer – 500g (cubed)	Heat the oil in a pan and add the onions and fry until starting to brown, then add the garlic & ginger paste and salt, mix well and cook for 2 minutes.
Onion – 2 (finely sliced)	
Tomato – 3 (finely chopped)	
Bell Pepper – 2 (red & green - chopped)	
Green Chilli - 3 (split)	Add the garam masala, chilli powder, coriander powder, cumin and turmeric, mix well and fry for 1 minute.
Ginger & Garlic Paste – 2 tbsp	
Heavy Cream – 1/2 cup	
Cashew Nut – ½ cup (boiled for 5 minutes and blended into a paste)	Next, add the tomatoes and cook until they have softened. Use a little water if the sauce dries out, and then add the bell pepper and the kasuri methi.
Garam Masala – 1 tsp	
Kasuri Methi – 1 tbsp	
Chilli Powder – 1 tsp	
Coriander Powder – 1 tbsp	Add the cashew nut paste along with the cream and allow to come to the boil, and then finally add the paneer and allow to simmer for 5 minutes.
Cumin Powder - 1 tsp	
Turmeric – 1 tsp	
Oil – 5 tbsp	
Salt - to taste	

Laal Maas

Rajasthan is a very dry region and due to the scarcity of vegetables meat dishes have been perfected over the centuries. Laal Maas literally translates as 'red mutton' and can also be cooked using goat. The authentic recipe requires the bright red chillies from the region of Mathania but of course you can use any dried red chillies at your disposal. There is also another variation of this recipe called 'jungli maas' which uses game meats instead of lamb or goat.

Ingredients

Lamb – 500g
Turmeric – 1 tsp
Garam Masala – 1 tsp
Coriander Powder – 2 tsp
Cumin Powder - 1 tsp
Yogurt – 1 cup
Ginger & Garlic Paste – 2 tbsp
Dried Red Chillies – 20-30 (deseeded)
Oil – 5 tbsp
Green Cardamom – 6
Cloves – 4
Cassia – 3" stick
Black Cardamom - 2
Bay Leaf - 2
Onion – 3 medium (finely chopped)
Ginger & Garlic Paste – 2 tbsp
Salt – to taste

Method

Soak the chillies with enough boiling water to cover them and allow to cool until the chillies has softened then blend them into a fine paste.

Heat the oil and add all the whole spices and cook for 1 minute.

Next, add the onions and fry slowly until golden brown and then add the ginger & garlic paste and cook for another minute.

Add the lamb and salt and fry until the edges of the meat have browned.

Next add the chilli paste and cook for 5 minutes. Add a little water if the pan dries.

Mix all the powdered spices with the yogurt and a little water then add it to the dish and stir well.

Finally, add enough water to cover the ingredients and cover the pot with a lid and simmer on a low heat for 1 hour. After cooking, the bones of the lamb should look clean (unless you are using boneless lamb) and the lamb will be tender.

RECIPES OF THE

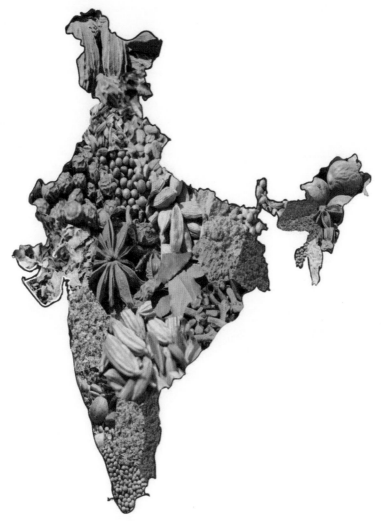

WESTERN REGION

Shaak

Due to the prevalence of the Jain religion, the majority of Gujatis are vegetarian and use hing/asafoetida powder as a substitute for onions and garlic. Shaak is the Gujarati word for 'vegetables' and this dish is a great vegetable dish where the vegetables can be changed accordingly to what is in season, or available. There are countless Shaark recipes some using only one vegetable.

Ingredients

Cumin Seed – 1 tbsp
Black Mustard Seed – 1 tbsp
Potato – 2 (cubed)
Cauliflower – 1/3 (florets)
Carrot – 1 (diced)
French Beans – 50g (chopped)
Peas – 1/2 cup
Small Aubergine – 1 (cubed)
Spinach – 1/2 cup (chopped)
Tomato – 2 (coarsely chopped)
Oil – 5 tbsp
Hing – 1/3 tsp
Green Chilli – 4 (split)
Turmeric – 1 tsp
Chilli Powder – 1 tsp
Garam Masala – 1 tsp
Salt – to taste
Jaggery/Sugar – ½ tsp

Method

Heat the oil in a pan and add the cumin and black mustard seed along with the hing powder.

Fry for a minute, and then add all of the vegetables (besides the tomatoes). Add a cup of water and stir.

Cover with a lid and simmer until the vegetables have softened (approximately 15 minutes).

Add the tomatoes, salt, jiggery, chilli powder and garam masala. Mix well and simmer for a further 7 minutes.

MAHARASHTRA

Chicken Manchurian

Chicken Manchurian can also be made by substituting chicken with paneer for a vegetarian version. Although Manchurian dishes originated in Maharashtra they have a strong influence from China due to both Manchuria and Maharashtra having a long history of trading that influenced the cuisine of the region. They types of dishes are known as Desi-Chinese or Indo-Chinese. Manchurian dishes have a sweet and sour sauce which can be used scarcely to create a dry version, or a gravy version by simply adding more water.

Ingredients	Method

Ingredients

Chicken breast – 500g
Corn Flour – 1 cup
Plain Flour – 3 tbsp
Chilli Powder – 1 tsp
Salt – to taste
Ginger & Garlic Paste – 2 tbsp
Water – as required
Oil – for deep frying

Gravy
Ginger – 2" piece (chopped)
Garlic – 5 cloves (chopped)
Onion – 2 (sliced)
Green Chilli – 4 (split)
Tomato Ketchup – 3 tbsp
Chilli Sauce – 3 tbsp
Soya Sauce - 3 tbsp
Green Bell Pepper – 2 (cubed)
Ground Black Pepper – ½ tsp
Brown Sugar - 1 tsp
Vinegar – 1 tbsp
Corn Flour – 3 tbsp (dissolved in ½ cup water)
Oil – 4 tbsp
Salt – to taste
Spring Onion – 1 bunch (chopped, white part for gravy, green part for garnish)

Method

In a bowl, mix the corn flour, plain flour, chilli powder, salt, ginger & garlic paste and add a little water to make a smooth batter. Then add the chicken and stir to coat the chicken in the batter.

Deep fry the coated chicken until golden brown and take it out with a slotted spoon and put onto kitchen paper to remove any excess oil and keep aside.

Gravy
Add the oil in a pan and add the ginger & garlic and fry briefly. Then add the white part of the spring onions, green pepper, green chilli and cook for 3 minutes.

Add soya sauce, ketchup, chilli sauce, black pepper, vinegar, sugar and salt, stir well and cook for 1 minute.

Finally, add the remaining corn flour mix, bring back to boil (add more water for a thinner sauce) and finally add the battered chicken, stir and bring to a boil. Garnish with the green part of the chopped spring onion.

King Fish Curry

Goan fish curry is made from any of the various fish that is caught locally including mackerel, snapper, or even prawns but king fish (the largest variety of mackerel) is very popular. Its fiery red colour from the ground spices gives an intense flavour and is traditionally served with white rice or semi-polished red rice.

Ingredients	Method
Kingfish – 500g	Heat 2 tbsp of coconut oil in a pan.
Fresh Coconut – 1 cup (grated)	
Tamarind Pulp – ¼ cup	Add the fish and fry for a couple of minutes each side until it is browned slightly, then remove the fish and set aside on a plate.
Fresh Ginger – 2" piece (peeled)	
Dried Red Chillies – 20	
Black Pepper Corns – 1 tbsp	
Cumin Seed – 1.5 tbsp	
Coriander Seed – 2.5 tbsp	Blend/grind all the remaining ingredients (besides the remaining 4 tbsp of coconut oil and salt) into a smooth paste adding a little water if necessary.
Turmeric – 1 tsp	
Green Chilli - 3	
Salt – to taste	
Virgin Organic Coconut Oil – 6 tbsp	

In the same pan as the fish was fried, heat the remaining 4 tbsp of coconut oil, then add the blended paste along with the salt and cook on a gentle simmer for 10 minutes to allow the spices to cook through.

Finally, add the fried fish and cook on a low flame for 10-15 minutes until the fish is softened.

RECIPES OF THE

SOUTHERN REGION

Bisi Bele Bath

Bisi Bele Bath is a delicious and hearty one pot combination of rice, lentils and vegetables that resembles a stew and is laden with spices with the addition of tamarind for a sour element. The choice of vegetables in the ingredients merely serves as a suggestion and can be changed according to availability and preference. This is a Jain version of the dish that has no onions or garlic but of course you can add them if you wish.

Ingredients	Method

Ingredients

Basmati Rice – 1 cup
Urid Dal – 1 cup (soaked for 3 hours)
Chana Dal – 1/2 cup (soaked overnight)
Salt – to taste
Turmeric – 1 tsp

The Masala
Dried Red Chilli – 3 pieces
Cassia – 2" stick
Cloves – 5
Tamarind – 2 tbsp
Jaggery/Sugar– 1 tsp
Fresh Shredded Coconut – ½ cup
Fenugreek Seed – 1 tbsp
Poppy Seed – 1 tbsp

Vegetables
Green Peas – 1/2 cup
Carrots – 1 medium (diced)
Green Beans – 1 cup
Green Peppers – 1 medium
Potato – 1 large (peeled and diced)

Tarka
Ghee – 3 tbsp
Curry Leaves – 30
Cashew Nuts – 3 tbsp (broken)
Hing – ¼ tsp
Black Mustard Seed – 1 tsp
Dried Red Chilli – 2 (broken)

Method

Dry roast all the ingredients in the 'masala' list and then blend into a fine powder.

Put the 'vegetables', chana & urid dal, salt, 'ground masala mix', turmeric, rice into a large pan and simmer for 15 minutes in enough water to cover the ingredients by about an inch.

In a separate pan, heat the ghee and gently fry all the remaining ingredients for the 'tarka', mix well until the mustard seed start to crackle and pour on top of the finished dish.

Royyala Vepudu

This dish makes excellent use of the local ingredients from the coastline and the abundance of spices that grow in the region. Although it is not over indulgent in spices which helps retain the flavour of the prawns. Royyala, even though it sounds like it may mean 'royal' in fact means shrimp/prawn in the Telugu language and Vepunda means 'fry'. The absence of tomatoes which i pretty common in southern Indian dishes means that this dish is slightly dry.

Ingredients

Prawns – 500g
Onion – 3 (finely sliced)
Ginger & Garlic Paste – 2 tbsp
Chilli Powder – 1 tsp
Turmeric Powder – 1 tsp
Green Chilli – 4 (split)
Fennel Powder – ½ tsp
Coriander Powder – 1 tbsp
Kasuri Methi – 1 tsp
Grated Fresh Coconut – 1 cup
Curry Leaves – 30
Garam Masala – 1/2 tsp
Salt – to taste

Method

Marinate the prawns for 30 minutes with the turmeric, salt and a little lemon juice.

Heat oil in a pan and add the onions, salt and fry until turning brown, then add the ginger & garlic paste and fry for a further 2 minutes.

Add the grated coconut, green chilli, fennel powder, coriander powder, mix well and fry for another 2 minutes along with half a cup of water.

Add the curry leaves, kasuri methi and the prawns and finally cook for 3 minutes until most of the water has evaporated, and finally add the garam masala and stir in to serve.

Chettinad Chicken

In the state of Tamil Nadu a region called Chettinad can be found that is renowned not just in South India but throughout the world for its amazing combination of well balanced spices and fresh tropical ingredients which are often ground into a paste before cooking. The philosophy of the community known as the Chettiars, or Nattukota is based heavily on their food and pleasing their dinner guests. Chettinad Chicken is one of the most renowned chicken dishes in India for good reason.

Ingredients	Method

Ingredients

Chicken – 500g
Onion – 2 medium (finely sliced)
Ginger & Garlic Paste – 2 tbsp
Tomatoes – 8 (chopped small)
Curry Leaves – 20 leaves
Sesame Oil (Gingelly Oil) – 4 tbsp
Salt – to taste

Spice Mix
Coriander Seed – 1 tbsp
Cumin Seed – 2 tsp
Poppy Seed – 1 tsp
Fennel Seed – 1 tsp
Black Pepper Corns – 1 tsp
Cassia – 2" stick
Black Mustard Seed – 1 tsp
Fenugreek Seed – 1 tsp
Cloves – 4
Dried Red Chilli – 10
Freshly Grated Coconut – 1 cup

Method

Dry roast all the ingredients in the 'spice mix' list, add the coconut last and toast it slightly.

Then, grind all the roasted ingredients into a smooth paste with a little water.

Heat the sesame oil in a pan and sauté the onions for a until starting to brown and then add the chicken along with the salt.

Once the onions and chicken are starting to brown, add the ginger & garlic paste and the curry leaves and fry for a further 2 minutes.

Add the tomatoes and cook until they start to disintegrate.

Then add the blended ingredients and simmer on a medium heat for 25 minutes with a lid on the pan until the chicken is tender. Add a little water if the sauce dries out while simmering.

Nadan Kozhi

Kerala has a long history of spice trading and has so much to offer in terms of its diverse and renowned food. Nadan Kozhi is a popular chicken dish which is simple to cook but bursting with flavour and best cooked using coconut oil.

Ingredients

Chicken – 500g
Ginger & Garlic Paste – 2 tbsp
Onions – 3 (sliced)
Green Chilli – 4 (split)
Curry Leaves – 30 leaves
Turmeric – 1 tsp
Coriander Powder – 1 tbsp
Chilli Powder – 1 tsp
Garam Masala – 1 tsp
Tomato – 2 (coarsely chopped)
Salt – to taste
Oil - 6 tbsp

Method

Heat the oil in a pan, and add the onions and fry until golden.

Next, add the ginger & garlic paste and fry gently for 1 minute.

Add the chicken and fry until it has browned on the edges.

Add the turmeric, chilli powder, coriander powder, turmeric, green chilli, curry leaves, salt and garam masala then stir well.

Finally, add the tomatoes and a cup and a half of water and simmer for 20 minutes with a lid on the pan.

Meen Kulambu

Meen Kulambu translated from Tamil as 'fish broth' is a delicious fish curry that offers the very best of the ingredients of the region. It is typically made using barracuda fish but goes excellently with any sea fish of your choice. Similar curries can be found in Kerala and in Bengali cuisine.

Ingredients	Method

Ingredients	Method
Fish – 500g	Mix the fish with salt, turmeric and ginger &
Garlic & Ginger Paste – 2 tbsp	garlic paste and marinate for 3 hours.
Onion – 2 (sliced thinly)	
Tomato – 3 (finely chopped)	Gather all the ingredients in the 'paste' list
Green Chilli – 3 (split)	and grind to a smooth paste with a little
Turmeric – 1 tsp	water.
Curry Leaves – 30	
Black Mustard Seed – 1 tsp	Heat oil in a pan and add the cumin, fenugreek
Fenugreek Seed – 2/3 tsp	& black mustard seed and cook for 1 minute.
Cumin Seed – ½ tsp	
Salt – to taste	Add the onions, and fry until brown. Then add
Tamarind Paste - 2 tbsp	the chilli, curry leaves and tomato and
Oil – 5 tbsp	simmer until the tomatoes have disintegrated.
Paste	Next add the paste along with the salt, stir
Coconut – 1 cup (shredded)	well and cook for 5 minutes on a medium
Coriander Seed – 1 tbsp	heat. Add water if dries out.
Fennel Seed – 1 tsp	
Dried Red Chilli – 2	Finally, add the marinated fish and cook
Cloves – 4	on a gentle flame for 15 minutes.
Green Cardamom – 4	
Cashew Nut – 40g	

Hyderabadi Biryani

Although there is a section on rice dishes in the book starting on page 117, this famous biryani dish deserves to be in the main recipe section as it is a complete meal in itself. Many people enjoy it with a simple bowl of cucumber raita, which is just some chopped cucumber in a plain yogurt sauce. Hyderabad is renowned for its food, especially its biryani which was introduced by the Persians/Parsis and is one of the most extravagant rice dishes in India. 'Birian' is the Persian word for 'fried before cooking' and 'birinj' is the Persian word for rice.

Ingredients	Method
Chicken Legs – 4	Marinate for chicken in all the 'marinade' ingredients for 3 hours and then add it to a pot with a lid on and cook it for 20 minutes.
Caramelised Onions – 3 (pre-fried slowly in oil)	

Marinade

Rice

Salt – to taste

Add the whole spices form the 'rice' list into 7 cups of water and bring to a boil. Then add the rice and continue to boil gently for 5 minutes before draining.

Garam Masala – 1 tsp
Ghee – 5 tbsp
Ginger & Garlic Paste – 1 tbsp
Chilli Powder – 2 tsp
Coriander Powder – 2 tbsp
Turmeric Powder – 1 tsp
Fresh Coriander – Small bunch
(finely chopped)

Layering

Now add the fried onions evenly on top of the chicken gravy and then add the parboiled rice evenly on top and level off your rice so that it is flat.

Yogurt – 200ml
Ghee – 4 tbsp
Water – 250ml
Saffron – 1 tsp (optional, can be substituted with ½ tsp turmeric)

Add a moderate sprinkle of warm water (including the saffron if you are using it) to your rice then place a lid on the pot and steam gently for a further 15 minutes. When the steaming is over, serve each portion with a piece of the chicken with a slotted spoon from the bottom of the pan to create varying colours of rice when plated.

Rice

Basmati Rice – 2 cups
Green Cardamom – 6
Cloves - 6
Cassia – 3" stick
Cumin Seed – 1 tbsp
Salt – to taste

RECIPES OF THE

CENTRAL REGION

Butter Chicken

Delhi is the capital city of India and was also the capital of the Mughal Empire and became the birthplace as what we now know of Mughlai cuisine. Delhi is a melting pot of people from all over India so its food has many different influences from the various cultures that have all helped to modify the food in unique ways. Butter Chicken is one of India's most iconic dishes and was invented by Kundan Lal Jaggi (1924 – 2018) who established the now popular Moti Mahal chain of restaurants and also invented Dal Makhani.

Ingredients	Method
Chicken Breast – 500g	Heat the ghee in a pan and fry the onions gently until starting to brown.
Yogurt – 150ml	
Ghee – 5 tbsp	
Salt – to taste	Next, add the ginger & garlic paste, stir and cook for 2 minutes.
Onions – 2 (finely sliced)	
Tomatoes – 5 (blended)	
Ginger & Garlic Paste – 2 tbsp	Add the chicken and stir well and cook until the chicken has browned.
Chilli Powder – 1 tbsp	
Coriander Powder – 2 tsp	
Cumin Powder – 1 tsp	Then add the powdered spices, salt, tomatoes and continue to simmer for 10 minutes, adding a little water.
Garam Masala – ½ tsp	
Salt – to taste	
Kasuri Methi – 1 tsp (plus more for garnish)	
Butter – 2 tbsp	Add the kasuri methi, butter, yogurt and the cream, stir well and allow to come to the boil and serve with a swirl of cream & sprinkle with finely chopped fresh coriander and a little kasuri methi.
Single Cream – 150ml (plus more for garnish)	
Fresh Coriander – to garnish	

Kakori Kebabs

Kakor is a town in the Lucknow district renowned for its kebabs which are a more refined version sheekh kebabs with a softer texture and flagrant flavour. Legend had it that a Nawabi (Mughlai) chef cooked some kebabs for a banquet in the 1920s and one of his British diplomatic guests mentioned that the kebabs were chewy. The chef took great offence and spent days and nights trying to come up with the perfect kebab which resulted in the creation of Kakori kebabs. You could also cook these kebabs on a barbeque.

Ingredients	Method
Lamb – 500g (minced, including approximately 150g of fat) Ginger & Garlic Paste – 2 tbsp Salt – to taste Chilli Powder – 1 tsp Tenderising Powder – ½ tsp (optional) Onions – 2 medium (finely sliced) Gram Flour – ¼ cup (dry roasted) Ghee – 2 tbsp (more for brushing while cooking) Garam Masala – 1 tbsp	Fry the onions with a little oil until golden brown and blend into a paste. Dry roast all the ingredients in the 'spice mix' list and grind into a coarse powder. Put the minced lamb into a bowl and add 'all' the remaining ingredients including the spice mix you have just ground.
Spice Mix Cloves – 4 Nutmeg – pea sized piece Black Pepper Corns – 1 tsp Mace – 2 blades Black Cardamom – 3 Green Cardamom – 6 Cassia - 2" stick Cumin seed - 1 tbsp	Mix well and allow to marinate for 3 hours. Shape the kebab meat around the skewers so they are roughly 1 inch in thickness and have a smooth surface. Place the kebabs in a preheated oven at 190 degrees centigrade until fully cooked and charring on the edges.
Garnish Lime Wedges – 1 lime cut into 4 Red Onion – 2 medium (sliced) Green Chutney - (see page 27)	Brush evenly with a few drips of ghee half way through cooking process. Turn your kebabs while cooking to ensure all sides are cooked.

Bhopali Ghost Korma

Bhopal is the capital city of Madhya and offers a wide range of meat dishes. Ghost korma is a hugely flavoursome lamb dish packed with spices but balanced in taste.

Ingredients

Lamb – 500g
Bay leaf - 2
Ginger & Garlic Paste – 2 tbsp
Turmeric Powder – 1 tsp
Salt – to taste
Chilli Powder – 1 tsp
Kewra Essence - a few drops
(optional)
Yogurt – 2 cups
Onions – 2 (finely chopped)
Oil – 4 tbsp

Spice Mix
Coriander Seed – 2 tbsp
Cumin Seed – 1 tsp
Fennel Seed – 1 tsp
Black Cardamom - 3
Black Pepper Corns - 10
Cassia - 2" stick
Star Anise – 1
Green Cardamom – 4
Nutmeg – 1 pinch
Mace – 3 blades

Method

Grind all the ingredients listed in the 'spice mix' into a fine paste.

Heat the oil in a pan and brown the lamb along with the onions (approximately 10 minutes).

Add the bay leaves along with the ginger & garlic paste, and onions, and cook for 15 minutes on a medium temperature adding water if pan runs dry.

Next, add the ground spice mix along with the turmeric, chilli powder, salt and yogurt along with a cup of water.

Bring to a boil and leave to simmer for 1 hour with a lid on the pan until the lamb has fully softened, adding water when necessary.

Add a few drops of kewra essence before serving.

Pakodi Ki Kadhi

This is a great vegetarian dish inspired by the Punjabi people of Chhattisgarh. It consists of a simplified but very tasty version of onion bhajis that sit on top of a thick spicy yogurt gravy (kadhi) with the addition of seasoned oil/tarka poured over the top for added flavour.

Ingredients	Method
Pakodi	**Pakodi**

Pakodi

Besan – 100g (sifted)
Onion – 2 (cut into thin strips)
Chilli Powder – 1 tsp
Green Chilli – 3 (thinly sliced)
Turmeric – 1 tsp
Salt – to taste
Oil – for deep frying

Kadhi

Yogurt – 2 cups
Onion – 2 (thinly sliced)
Coriander Powder – 1 tbsp
Chilli Powder – 1 tsp
Turmeric – 1 tsp
Cumin Powder – 1 tsp
Ginger & Garlic Paste – 2 tbsp
Gram Flour – 1/3 cup (dry roasted until browned)
Ajwain – ½ tsp
Garam Masala – ½ tsp
Salt – to taste
Oil - 3 tbsp

Seasoned Oil

Ghee - 3 tbsp
Cumin Seed – 1 tsp
Onion Seed – 1 tsp
Chilli Powder – 1 tsp

Method

Pakodi

Mix all the ingredients in the 'pakodi' list (besides the oil) and use a little water to make a firm batter. Then add the onions and mix well.

Divide the onion batter into balls roughly the size of a lime and deep fry until golden brown.

Remove the pakodis from the oil then drain any excess oil and keep aside to add to the gravy/kadhi.

Kadhi

Heat the oil then fry the onions until starting to brown, then add the ginger & garlic paste and fry for 2 minutes.

Add all the powdered ingredients along with the salt, ajwain and cook for 2 minutes then add the yogurt and mix well adding a little water if necessary to create a smooth paste.

Seasoned Oil

Heat the ghee and add the cumin and black seed until they crackle then turn off the heat and stir in the chilli powder.

To Serve

Put the gravy into a serving boil, add the pakodi and pour the seasoned oil evenly over the top.

RECIPES OF THE

EASTERN REGION

Chingri Malai

Chingri Malai is a popular Bengali dish that was also favoured by the British during the time of the Raj. The dish offers the best flavours of the coast-line and the makes use of the abundant spices and coconuts that grow in the region.

Ingredients

Big Prawns – 500g
Lime Juice – 1 lime
Onions – 2 medium (finely sliced)
Cumin Seed – 1 tbsp
Cloves – 6
Green Cardamom – 6
Cassia – 2" stick
Dried red Chilli – 2
Bay Leaf – 2
Ginger & Garlic Paste – 2 tbsp
Turmeric – 1 tsp
Chilli Powder - tsp
Garam Masala – 1 tsp
Yogurt – ½ cup
Coconut Milk – 350ml/ 1 can
Salt – to taste
Mustard Oil – 6 tbsp
Fresh Coriander – 2 tbsp

Method

Marinate the prawns with the lime juice, turmeric and a pinch of salt for 30 minutes.

Heat 2 tbsp of mustard oil in a pan and fry the prawns for 2 minutes, stirring to ensure even cooking. Take the prawns out of the pan and leave aside for later.

In the same pan, add the remaining 4 tbsp of mustard oil and allow to heat. Then add all the whole spices and fry on a medium heat for 2 minutes.

Fry the onions until they become soft.

Add the ginger & garlic paste along with the powdered spices, salt and stir then fry for 2 minutes.

Add the yogurt and the coconut milk, mix well and simmer for a few minutes or until the sauce has thickened.

Add the cooked prawns, stir and simmer for a further 1 minute.

Lamb Salaan

Jharkhand is known as The Land of the Forest and its cuisine is influenced by its Mughlai invaders and although Islam forms about 15% of its population, meat dishes are common. Adding potatoes to meat dishes is common throughout East India and Lamb Salaan a relatively simple dish with few ingredients but is certainly very tasty.

Ingredients	Method
Lamb – 500g Potato – 350g (peeled & cubed) Onion – 3 (finely sliced) Tomato – 4 (chopped) Green Chilli – 4 (split) Garlic & Ginger Paste – 2 tbsp Turmeric– 1 tsp Oil – 5 tbsp Salt – to taste Garam Masala – 1 tbsp	Marinate the lamb with 'half' the onions, the garam masala powder and ginger & garlic paste then marinade for 3 hours. Heat the oil in a pan and add the remaining half of the onions and fry until browned. Add the lamb along with all the ingredients it was marinated in along with the potato, tomatoes, chillies, salt, garam masala and turmeric. Stir well and simmer with 2-3 cups of water until the potatoes are cooked and the lamb is tender (approximately 1 hour 15 minutes).

Reshmi Kebabs

Reshmi kebabs were introduced into the region by Mughlai invaders. Reshmi literally means 'silky' which explains the refined ingredients and cooking method which creates highly sumptuous kebabs. You could also cook these kebabs on a barbeque.

Ingredients

Chicken Pieces – 500g (boneless)
Thick Cream – 1 cup
Yogurt – 1 cup
Ginger & Garlic Paste – 2 tbsp
Cashew Nut Powder – 40g
Almond Powder – 40g
Ground Black Pepper - 1 tbsp
Lemon Juice - ½ a lemon
Coriander Powder – 1 tbsp
Cumin Powder- 1 tsp
Salt – to taste
Butter – to garnish (plus more for brushing while cooking)
Raw Red Onion – to garnish

Method

Marinate the chicken with all the ingredients (besides the butter) overnight.

Preheat your oven on the highest heat for 15 minutes.

Put the marinated chicken onto skewers and bake in the oven at approximately 190 degree centigrade until the chicken is cooked through and starting to char on the edges. Brush with a little oil while cooking.

Brush with melted butter to serve and garnish with red onion. Enjoy with green chutney (see page 27).

Doi Maach

Bengali cuisine is known for its rich array of flavours and seafood dishes. Doi Maach is a popular and traditional fish curry in the region (usually carp fish is used but you can change this accordingly to your taste of what is avaibale) cooked in an aromatic yogurt gravy with a little sweetness added from the use of jaggery.

Ingredients	Method
Fish – 500g	Marinate the fish for 3 hours in the yogurt, turmeric, coriander, jaggery and salt.
Onion – 3 (blended into a paste)	
Ginger & Garlic Paste – 2 tbsp	
Yogurt – 1 cup	
Green Chilli – 3 (split)	Heat the oil in a pan and fry the bay leaf, cloves, cumin seed, cassia and star anise for 2 minutes.
Coriander Powder – 1 tbsp	
Turmeric – 1 tsp	
Bay Leaf – 2	
Cloves – 5	Then add the onion paste and stir well until browned on a low heat, add a little water if the pan dries.
Cumin Seed – 2 tsp	
Cassia – 2" stick	
Jaggery/Sugar – 1 tsp	
Star Anise - 1	Next add the marinated fish along with the green chilli and continue to simmer for 15 minutes.
Salt – to taste	
Oil – 6 tbsp	

RECIPES OF THE

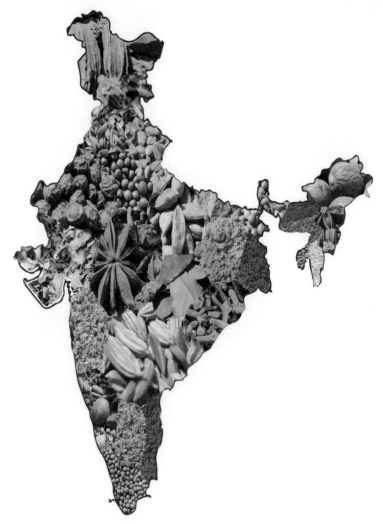

NORTH EASTERN REGION

Vegetable Thukpa

Like much of the dishes found in the North East of India they often differ greatly from the rest of India as they often have their roots in Central Asia. This mildly spicy noodle and vegetable soup has a strong influence from Nepalese cuisine and is very popular in Sikkim. You can use absolutely any noodles you like (rice noodles etc) or even spaghetti. The vegetables can also be changed to what is available.

Ingredients

Egg Noodles – 300g
Ginger – 2 " piece (chopped)
Onion – 1 (finely chopped)
Cabbage – 100g (shredded)
Carrots – 2 medium (grated)
Green Beans – 150g
Dried Red Chilli – 3 (broken)
Tomato – 2 (chopped)
Cumin Powder – ½ tsp
Black Pepper – 1/3 tsp
Garlic – 4 cloves (bashed)
Green Bell Pepper – 1 (sliced)
Turmeric – 1 tsp
Coriander Stalk – 50g (chopped)
Garam Masala – 1 tbsp
Lemon Juice – ½ a lemon
Salt – to taste
Light Soya Sauce – 1 tbsp
Oil – 4 tbsp

Garnish
Fresh Coriander, Chopped Red
Onion & Spring Onion.

Method

Heat the oil in a pan and add the onions, garlic, ginger and cook until starting to brown.

Then add the turmeric, broken chilli, garam masala, cumin, pepper and fry for a further 2 minutes.

Next, add the, carrots cabbage, green beans, and salt with just enough water to cover and simmer for 10 minutes.

Finally, add the noodles, coriander stalk, bell pepper, lemon juice, soya sauce and simmer for 15 minutes.

Add the 'garnish' to serve.

Doh Sniag Nei Long

Meghalayan cuisine is unique and different to its Northern neighbours. This spicy meat Doh Sniag Nei Long or Khasi pork curry (named after the Khasi tribe) is a popular pork dish. Don't be put off by the unusual black sauce as it is made from ground black sesame seed which gives an amazing warm taste.

Ingredients	Method

Ingredients

Pork – 500g (diced with fat)
Tomato – 3 (finely chopped)
Black Sesame Seed – 100g
(ground into paste with water)
Fresh Ginger – 3" piece
Garlic – 4 cloves
Green Chilli – 6
Onion – 3 (finely sliced)
Ground Black Pepper – 1 tsp
Bay Leaf – 2
Turmeric – 2 tsp
Oil – 4 tbsp
Salt – to taste

Method

Blend the onion, ginger, garlic and chilli into a coarse paste with a little water.

Boil the pork and salt for 20 minutes. Strain the water off with a colander but keep the water (stock) for later.

Add oil to a pan and fry the pork until it has browned, then add the 'onion, ginger, garlic and chilli paste' you made earlier along with the bay leaves and cook for 7 minutes on a medium heat.

Next add the tomatoes and cook until they have fully softened.

Then add the pepper, turmeric and sesame paste along with the pork 'stock' and simmer on a gentle heat for 20 minutes adding a little water if the pan dries out.

Masor Tenga

Assamese cuisine comprises a mixture of indigenous cooking styles. Masor Tenga is a relatively simple but surprisingly delicious tangy fish curry that is traditionally made with freshwater fish such as trout, catfish or perch but you can substitute with any fish you like.

Ingredients

Fish – 500g
Fenugreek Seed – 1 tsp
Ginger & Garlic Paste – 2 tbsp
Onions – 2 (finely sliced)
Potatoes – 2 (coarse cubes)
Tomatoes – 4 (cut into quarters)
Green Chilli – 2 (slit)
Turmeric Powder – 1 tsp
Lime Juice – 2 limes
Salt – to taste
Fresh Coriander – 1 tbsp
Mustard Oil – 6 tbsp

Method

Boil the potato along with the tomato with just enough water to cover them until the potatoes have softened (approximately 12 minutes), Drain the water off with a colander keep aside the water they were boiled in (stock).

Fry the fish both sides in the mustard oil until each side is sealed.

Take the fish out of the oil and put aside for later. Then heat up the fenugreek seed in the same oil in the same pan until they turn a reddish brown colour.

Add the onions and cook until starting to brown and then add the ginger & garlic paste and cook for 2 minutes.

Add the turmeric powder, salt and green chillies and stir in.

Next, add the potato and tomato along with the saved 'stock' and bring back to a boil.

Finally, add the fish and the lime juice and allow to simmer for 7 minutes with a lid on the pan.

Chicken Thukpa

This is a very similar dish to vegetable thukpa but with slightly more Chinese influence and with the addition of chicken. There are many varieties of thukpa but this is a winner for anyone who loves a great chicken noodle soup. The recipes calls for rice noodles but they can be substituted by another type of noodles depending on what is available.

Ingredients	Method

Stock
Chicken – 500g (shredded)
Onion – 2 (coarsely chopped)
Garlic – 5 cloves (whole)
Water – 1 litre
Salt – to taste

Paste
Onion – 1
Tomato – 2
Fresh Coriander – 20g
Ginger – 1"piece
Green Chilli – 2
Szechuan Pepper – 1 tsp
Oil - 2 tbsp

Other Ingredients
Rice Noodles – 400g
Red Pepper – 1 (cut into juliennes)
Cabbage – 100g (shredded)
Carrot – 1 (cut into juliennes)

Boil all the ingredients in the 'stock' list for 20 minutes. Then drain the ingredients but keep the water for later (stock).

Blend all the ingredients in the 'paste' list (besides the oil) into a fine paste and fry it in the oil for 5 minutes.

Add the fried paste to the stock ingredients along with the noodles, red pepper and carrot and simmer for 10 minutes along with the stock.

Naga Pork & Bamboo Shoots

The food of Nagaland reflects the Naga people who are descendents of Tibet Myanmar ethnic groups. The predominant religion of Nagaland is Christia hence, pork is very popular. The use of vegetables such as bamboo shoots ar very common in the region. The original recipe calls for fermented bambo shoots but fresh or tinned work fine. Nagaland is famous for its fiercely hot re chillies but you can substitute the type of chilli to what is available. Scotc bonnet chillies are a good alternative.

Ingredients	Method

Ingredients

Pork – 500g (chunks)
Fresh Red Chillies - 2
Tomato – 3
Bamboo Shoots – 100g
Onion – 2 (coarsely chopped)
Ginger & Garlic Paste – 2 tbsp
Salt – to taste
Oil – 3 tbsp

Method

Boil the pork in 1 litre of water along with salt until the water has evaporated. Between 40 minutes to 1 hour.

Blend the chillies and the tomato into a smooth paste.

Heat the oil and gently fry the pork and the onions until starting to brown.

Add the ginger & garlic paste and cook for 2 minutes.

Next, add the blended 'chilli and the tomato paste' and mix well.

Stir in the bamboo shoots and cook for a further 5 minutes until softened.

Yen Thongba

Manipuri cuisine is represented by the cuisine of the Meitei people who have origins in the central plains of Asia. Yen Thongba is a deliciously spicy chicken and potato dish typically served with white rice and a simple salad.

Ingredients	Method
Chicken – 500g	Heat the oil and add the black pepper, cassia, bay leaves, cumin seed, cardamom, fennel and fry for 2 minutes.
Cassia – 2" stick	
Cumin Seed – 1 tbsp	
Bay Leaf - 2	
Fennel Seed – 1 tsp	Add the onion along with the ginger & garlic, stir well, and cook until the onions have browned slightly. Then add the chicken and fry until it has browned.
Ground Black Pepper – ½ tsp	
Green Cardamom – 5	
Onion – 2 (sliced)	
Garlic & Ginger Paste – 2 tbsp	
Potato – 3 (cut in half & par-boiled)	Add the tomato, along with the green chilli, turmeric, coriander and salt.
Green Peas – 1 cup	
Tomato – 3 (chopped)	After stirring for 5 minutes (or, until the tomato has softened), add the peas and potato and simmer for 5 minutes before adding the garam masala 1 minute before serving.
Green Chilli – 4	
Turmeric – 1 tsp	
Coriander Powder – 1 tbsp	
Garam Masala – ½ tsp	
Salt – to taste	
Oil – 5 tbsp	

Panch Phoron Bai

Bai is a popular and simple one pot dish from Mizoram and is made from seasonal vegetables so recipes can differ greatly. The original recipe requires fermented soya beans which are not always easy to procure so they can be omitted, or regular soya beans can be used. The addition of panch phoron is a typical spice combination throughout the Bengali region which adds a delicious kick to the dish.

Ingredients

Pumpkin – 150g (chunks)
Aubergine – 1 (chunks)
Whole Okra – 100g
Potatoes – 200g (peeled & diced)
Cauliflower – 1/3 (florets)
White Rice – 1/3 cup
Salt - to taste
Bicarbonate of Soda - ½ tsp
Mustard Oil – 3 tbsp

Panch Phoron

Cumin Seed – 1 tbsp
Black Mustard Seed – 2 tsp
Fennel – 2 tsp
Fenugreek – 2 tsp
Nigella Seed – 2 tsp

Method

Heat the oil and add all the spices in the 'panch phoron' list and fry gently until the fenugreek seeds turn slightly red.

Then add 3-4 cups of water, the salt along with the rice and bicarbonate of soda.

When the water comes to a boil add the vegetables and simmer until the vegetables have softened and most of the water has been evaporated (approximately 20 -25 minutes).

Wahan Mosdeng

Wahan Mosdeng, or 'Chilli Pork' can be served as a main course but goes great as a simple side dish as it is very similar to a salad. The pork is scented with ginger and also has the additional flavour of roasted green chilli paste which makes the dish super tasty. The red onions and coriander are added raw and tossed into the pork.

Ingredients	Method
Pork – 500g Fresh Ginger – 3" piece (finely sliced) Red Onions – 2 medium (sliced into juliennes) Green Chilli – 10 Salt – to taste Fresh Coriander - ½ cup (chopped)	Boil the pork along with the ginger and salt with enough water to cover the pork and boil until tender, approximately 1 hour. Dry roast the green chillies in a pan. Once roasted, grind into a smooth paste using a little water if necessary. Add the pork and ginger to a bowl after discarding the water then add the chilli paste along with the onions, coriander and mix well.

ROTI (BREAD) RECIPES

CHAPATI

Chapati, also known as roti are simple to make are great for dipping into curries and dals and even making wraps with for kebabs.

Ingredients

Atta Flour – 200g (extra for rolling out)
Water – 100ml (approximately)
Salt – to taste

*Serve buttered (optional)

Method

Mix all the ingredients together in a bowl until you have formed a coarse dough. Knead the dough on a surface until elastic and no longer sticky.

Divide the dough into lime sized balls and cover with a tea-towel and allow to rest for 10 minutes.

Heat a flat surfaced frying pan (tava/crepe pan) and roll each of the dough balls into 3mm thick disks.

Cook one at a time on the hot pan. Cook on the first side until bubbles appear and then turn it over and cook on the over side until dark brown spots appear on both sides. Optionally, place the chapati in the open flame for a couple of seconds for it to puff up.

PARATTA

Paratta is a layered flaky bread that is great for dipping into dals and curries. The layers are achieved by how the dough is rolled out and also by adding little butter or ghee in the rolling process. This illustration shows 4 types of paratta. Clockwise from the top: A cauliflower mixture mixed in with the dough and fried both sides. 2; layered paratta (recipe to follow). 3; stuffed alu (potato) paratta. 4; stuffed paratta cooked with no oil.

PLAIN PARATTA

Ingredients

Flour – 2 cups (either atta or plain)
Ghee – 2 tbsp
Salt – to taste

Method

Mix the flour and salt with enough water to make a soft but firm dough. Knead the dough until slightly elastic and then allow to rest for 25 minutes.

Divide to dough into lemon sized balls. Spread a little ghee on a surface for rolling the dough out. Roll each ball out into an oblong shape around 2mm in thickness.

Apply a light dusting of flour and drizzle a little ghee onto each disk.
Next, fold the disk in 3 and stretch it until it is long but doesn't snap. Now coil the dough up into a roll shape.

Roll out the with a rolling pin so it is approximately 3mm in thickness and apply a little more ghee.

Heat a tava and add a little ghee and then add the paratta and cook both sides until starting to turn golden brown adding a little more ghee if necessary.

Once you have made all the parattas place them on top of each other and bash them a few times with your hand from the sides to help separate the layers.

ALU/ GOBI PARATTA

Alu (potato) or gobi (cauliflower) paratta is a fried, or 'not-fried' bread with a mildly spiced filling that goes great with curries and dals.

Ingredients

Flour – 2 cups (plain or atta)
Potato – 250g (boiled and mashed.
If using cauliflower grate it raw)
Ginger & Garlic Paste – 1 tbsp
Green Chilli – 2 (finely chopped)
Chilli Powder – 1 tsp
Fresh Coriander – Small handful
(finely chopped)
Garam Masala – 1 tsp
Turmeric – ½ tsp
Salt - to taste
Oil – for frying (optional)

Method

Mix the flour with enough water to make a firm dough and allow to rest for 15 minutes.

Mix all the remaining ingredients (besides the oil) into the mashed potato. Divide the dough into lemon sized balls.

Roll the dough out on a dusted surface into 7" wide circles. Add some of the spicy mashed potato mixture into the centre of the dough circles.

Turn the edges of the dough to meet in the centre to seal the dough around the mixture.

Twist tight to seal and carefully roll out each pirate onto a flour dusted surface. Cook both sides on a tava with some oil/ghee, or you can simply cook them without any oil/ghee for a healthier but less tasty option.

PURI

Puri can be made from either white or brown flour and are deep fried bread that is puffed up in the cooking process that go great with a wide range of curries and dals. Puri goes particularly well with vegetable curries. Hence, many people choose to eat chapatti with meat curries as they are lighter.

Ingredients

Atta Flour – 1 cup
Semolina – 1 tbsp
Oil – 1 tsp
Water – 60 to 70ml
Salt – to taste
Oil – for deep frying

Tip
Check the oil is hot enough by pinching a tiny bit of the dough and dropping it into the oil. If it rises to the surface within 3 seconds your oil is ready.

Method

Mix all the ingredients together (besides the oil) and briefly knead into a firm dough. Heat up the oil to a medium heat for deep frying & Divide the dough into 8 balls and roll out into round disks approximately 2-3 mm thick.

Slide a puri into the oil and press it down with a metal spoon to puff the puri (this should take about 5 seconds), and the carefully splash some oil onto the top with the spoon for a few seconds before taking out of the oil and placing onto some kitchen paper to drain the excess oil.

Cook each puri one at a time and serve.

AMRITSA KULCHA

Amritsa kulcha is one of the most ultimate Indian bread recipes, named after Amritsa, a city in the Punjab. It is stuffed with a mildly spices potato filling similar to alu parratta but is topped with chopped coriander leaf, crushed coriander seed and melted butter. It is the ideal accompaniment to Dal Makhani (see page 38) but goes great with any type of dal or curry. A little time consuming to make but worth the effort. Traditionally it is baked in a tandoor oven but can easily be made in a conventional oven.

Ingredients	Method

Roti
Plain Flour - 1.5 cups
Baking Soda – 1 tsp
Yogurt – 30g
Milk – 1/5 cup
Ghee – 1 tbsp

Filling
Potatoes - 100g (par-boiled & mashed)
Onion – 1 medium (finely chopped)
Fresh Coriander – small handful (finely chopped)
Green chillies – to taste (finely chopped)
Ginger & Garlic Paste – 1 tbsp
Ajwain seed 1/3 tsp
Cumin Powder - 2/3 tsp
Coriander Powder – 1.5 tsp
Chilli Powder – to taste
Salt – to taste
Ghee – 1.5 tsp (more for cooking/garnish)

Mix all the 'roti' ingredients and form a dough ball and let it rest, cover with a cloth while the filling is cooked.

Add the ghee to a pan and all the powdered spices along with the ajwain and ginger & garlic paste.

Next, add the onion and fry until browned, and then add the green chilli, salt, and mix well and then allow to cool. Then stir in the mashed boiled potato.

Divide the roti dough into lime sized balls, and roll out into disks roughly 5mm in thickness on a dusted surface.

Place some of the 'filling' mixture into the middle of each bread disk and work the dough around the potato mixture to seal, and then roll out carefully into stuffed disks.

Roll the chopped fresh coriander and cracked coriander seed onto the top of each roti then place into a preheated oven of 180 degrees until golden brown. Brush with a little butter/ghee to serve.

RICE ROTI

Rice roti is similar to a chapati but instead of atta flour *rice flour* is used.

Ingredients

Rice Flour – 1 cup (plus more for rolling out)
Water – 1 cup
Oil – 1 tbsp
Salt – to taste

Tip
Rice roti is a great alternative to other types of atta based breads are it is gluten free.

Method

Heat the water, salt & rice flour in a pan & mix well. Once it comes to a boil turn the heat off and allow the rice dough to cool.

Apply some addition rice flour to a surface and knead the dough until you have a smooth ball (approximately 5 minutes).

Allow the dough ball to rest for 10 minutes and then divide the dough into lime sized balls.

Heat a tava/dry flat pan and roll out each ball into circles of around 2-3mm in thickness. Cook both sides until each side has dark spots and serve warm.

CHAWAL (RICE) RECIPES

PLAIN RICE

Most curries are served with rice. Many people find rice difficult to cook correctly mainly due to the poor instructions on the packets by the manufacturer. Some say that you can judge a cook by the way they cook their rice so it is an important skill to master.

Ingredients

Method

Rice – 1 cup = 2 servings
Salt – to taste
Lemon Juice - Dash
Oil – Dash

Tips for ALL Rice Dishes
Pour the rice into a bowl and run the rice under cold water until the water is clear and then allow to soak for 30 minutes.

Never boil rice, allow it to gently simmer.

Puff the rice up with a folk only after it has been drained and rested.

Add the rice to a pan and add enough water to cover the rice by a couple of inches and add the lemon, salt and oil and bring to a boil.

Then turn the temperature down so the water only bubbles gently.

As soon as the rice doubles in size, simmer for a further 2 minutes.

Drain the water from the rice with a coriander and allow to rest for 10-15 minutes.

PILAU RICE

Pilau Rice is a fragrant and mildly spicy rice preparation that goes great with any Indian meal. This recipe provides a basic but quality pilau but of course there are many variations. You can simply change the recipe by adding peas, and/or any of your favourite vegetables which can be par-boiled beforehand.

Ingredients

Basmati Rice – 2 cups
Onions – 2 (finely sliced)
Ginger & Garlic Paste – 1 tbsp
Green Cardamom – 5
Cassia – 3" stick
Cloves – 6
Mace – 2 blades
Cumin Seed – 1 tsp
Saffron – ¼ g (use ½ tsp of turmeric as a substitute)
Salt – to taste
Oil – 3 tbsp

Tip
If you are using saffron, soak it in ½ cup of hot water or milk for 10 minutes.

Method

Heat the oil and fry the whole spices for 2 minutes on a medium heat. Then add the onions and once browned add the ginger & garlic paste and cook for 2 minutes.

Add the rice, turn the heat down to a minimum and stir the rice carefully. Once mixed well, add 4 cups of hot water, then add the saffron water.

Adjust the temperature so that the rice simmers (not boils). Cover with a lid and cook for 10-12 minutes (all the water should have absorbed into the rice).

Turn off the heat, and allow to rest without a lid for 10 minutes.

OTHER PUBLICATIONS & PRODUCTS

Steven Heap Recipes on YouTube

This channel started back in 2016 and now has millions of views and offers over 900 video recipes, travel blogs, restaurant visits and reviews.

Link: youtube.com/stevenheaprecipes

Steven Heap on Instagram

For YouTube video recipe food pictures and travel pictures.

Link: instagram.com/steven.heap

Taste of India Spices

For all your Indian food spice needs visit 'Taste of India Spices' on eBay where you can purchase all your premium quality Whole and Powdered spices as well as highly popular Spice Blends that are all freshly roasted and ground to order for superior taste and aroma.

Link: ebay.co.uk/usr/toi_spices

Free UK Delivery and World Wish Shipping available. Send inquiries for world-wide shipping & enquiries.

OTHER BOOKS AVAILABLE AT AMAZON

British Indian Restaurant Food at Home

By Steven Heap

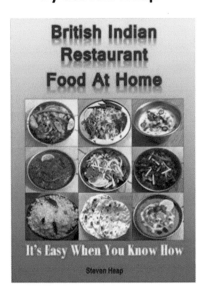

Authentic South Indian Cuisine

By Steven Heap

ABOUT THE AUTHOR

Although Steven Heap is native British his first experience of Indian food was in his family home. His grandfather had served in India towards the end of the Second World War and returned to England with a few recipes he had been given. His grandfather would cook a curry every Friday night which then inspired Steven's mother with her love of Indian food. At the age of 14 he got a part-time job washing up and prepping vegetables at an Indian restaurant where he expanded his food knowledge.

After going away to university in London in the early 2000s he lived at various lodgings including Pakistani and Indian homes where he cooked side by side with the residents. He began to fall in love with the food from South Asia and quickly incorporated it into his daily diet.

After graduating from university he first visited India to further explore his food interests. This was the start of many trips to Asia in his quest for food inspiration. In 2008 he moved to Malaysia which has a large Indian community and made regular trips all over Asia including Sri Lanka *and of course* to explore more of the food culture that India has to offer.

By this time he had become accomplished in the Indian kitchen and returning to the UK went on to cook at several British restaurants and also offered cookery classes. His creativity was noticed and he was invited to cook for the famous music star Wiz Khalifa on European tours which inspired the confidence to write 2 Indian food books and start a YouTube channel showcasing his dishes. Steven also regularly competes in cookery competitions against industry standard chefs and has never places less then third position, and in 2018 qualified for the World Culinary Cup in Luxembourg representing the UK in the Indian category.

Steven's unique and varied insight into Indian food combined with his passion for spreading the popularity of this cuisine was his goal in writing this book and he has dedicated himself to become a lifelong student of Indian cuisine and wants to inspire others.

GLOSSARY

Descriptions and Hindi translations for common cookery associated words.

Ingredients

Almond, badam
Aubergine, brinjal, egg plant
Beef, meat
Bell pepper, capsicum
Bread, roti, chapati, naan
Butter, makhani
Carrot, gajur
Cashew, gaju
Cauliflower, gobi
Chana dal – dried chickpeas
Chicken, murgh
Chickpeas, chana, garbonzo
Coconut, nariyal
Cream , malai
Fish, machalee
Food, khana
Garlic, lahasan
Ginger, andrak
Keema, minced/ground meat
Lamb, mutton, gosht
Masala, spice mix, gravy
Okra, bhindi, ladies fingers
Onion, pyaz
Paratta, parotha, prata
Popadoms, padad, appalam
Prawn, jhingha
Spinach, saag, palaak
Tamarind, imli, imalee
Vegetables, sabzi
Vinegar, siraka
Water, pani
Wheat Flour, atta
Plain/all-purpose flour, maida
Yogurt, curd, dahee

Herbs & Spices

Bay leaf (often confused with tej patta)
Black salt (sour pink coloured salt)
Black seed, wild onion seed, kalonji,
Kalwanji
Cardamom, elaichi
Chaat masala, sour spice mix
Chilli, mirch
Cloves, lavang
Coriander, dhaniya
Cumin, jeera, zeera
Fennel, saunf
Fenugreek leaves, kasuri methi
Fenugreek seed, methi eke beej
Fenugreek, methi
Leaf, patta
Mace, javantri (nutmeg's outer
membrane)
Mango powder, amchaar
Mustard, saraso
Nutmeg, jaayaphal
Powder, pauder
Saffron, zafron
Salt, namak
Screw pine, kewra
Seeds, beej
Star anise, chakr phool
Tej Patta, cinnamon leaf
Turmeric, haldi

Colours

Black, kala
Green, hara
Red, lal
White, saphed

Printed in Great Britain
by Amazon

37054877R00078